The Sounds of Chaucer's English

A Study Pamphlet and Script to
Accompany an Instructional Recording

Prepared by Daniel Knapp
and Niel K. Snortum
San Francisco State College

NATIONAL COUNCIL OF TEACHERS OF ENGLISH

THE SOUNDS OF CHAUCER'S ENGLISH

One album of three records with one pamphlet..$4.95
    Stock No. RL20-8

One pamphlet without record album...$1.50
    Stock No. P56-122

Five or more pamphlets...$1.00 each
    Stock No. P56-122

THE SOUNDS OF CHAUCER'S ENGLISH

OUTLINE

THE SOUNDS OF CHAUCER'S ENGLISH

BACKGROUNDS

Middle English is the earliest period of English that you can expect to learn without the special concentration needed to learn a foreign language. It is also the key to the richest store of poetry before Shakespeare—*Gawain and the Green Knight, Piers Plowman*, the Wakefield Plays, and Geoffrey Chaucer. Fortunately Chaucer's dialect is the easiest kind of Middle English for us to learn, since it became the basis for modern Standard English—for reasons that had almost nothing to do with Chaucer. In fact, once you have learned a small group of Middle English inflections and a larger group of special words or special meanings for familiar words, about the only thing that stands in the way of your becoming a fluent reader of Chaucer's English is its phonology, or sound system. For between Chaucer and us stands the "Great Vowel Shift," which changed the pronunciation of about half the words in the language.

Our purpose is to help you become a fluent reader of Chaucer's English, and this recording and its accompanying booklet are designed for that objective. They do not act as an introduction to general linguistics, although a number of the principles used and discussed have general application, and modern linguistic science lies behind our method. They do not act as a history of the English language, but we do draw on Old English for some explanations and point to Modern English for some helpful hints. They do not even act as an introduction to Middle English, for we say almost nothing about any but Chaucer's dialect, and we have emphasized the sounds of Chaucer's English much more strongly than his vocabulary and word formation, morphology, and syntax. On the other hand, a few remarks from the standpoint of each of these studies—general language study, history of English, and Middle English itself—will help to put Chaucer's English into its context.

1. *General Language Study*

To begin with, we must remember that Chaucer's English, like any language, was a structure of sounds (what we in English call "words") conventionally connected by a culture to patterns of experience (a connection that we summarize by the term "meaning").

Chaucer's language, then, was spoken, and it was subject to the same sort of forces that we can observe at work in our own speech. Because his language, like ours, responded to the needs of the culture it expressed, it provided him with a richly differentiated vocabulary of arms, hunting, chivalric conduct, courtly love, astrology, and alchemy, to take only a few examples, much as ours gives us a well-developed vocabulary for technology, sport, and the modern arts of love. It was a language based, like ours, chiefly on what people said and not on what people wrote, read, or taught. In fact, Chaucer apparently had reading aloud in mind even when he was writing, for he speaks in *Troilus and Criseyde* of times when his verse might be "read or sung." And like ours, his language was subject to two conflicting tendencies: on the one hand, it was a part of conventional behavior and thus tended to be conservative and static; on the other, it was the property of a group of human beings engaged in many kinds of development and change and therefore tended to be changeable, as dress and etiquette are. These antagonistic motives have their counterparts in our modern point of view toward Chaucer's English. We see much that has remained static and thus is immediately recognizable—though much that looks familiar may sound unfamiliar. But we also see much that has changed and has come to seem foreign, and shortly it will be clear that some of Chaucer's English is more foreign than it seems.

2. *History of English: through Old English*

Chaucer's English is the inheritor of a thousand years of change and borrowing in English alone and of eons of development before English even existed as a separate language. Much of this process we know only by reconstruction and hypothesis, for writing is a recent art. Several thousand years before the beginning of the Christian Era, in Eurasian lands somewhere between the Baltic and the Steppes, a group developed who spoke a language we hypothetically call Indo-European. (You may also hear it called Indo-Hittite.) They probably said something like *leuk* for "light," *reg* for "king," and *nem* or *nom* for "name." As the centuries went on, some parts of the group moved as far apart as Norway and India, and their linguistic descendents peopled most of modern Europe, Russia, Iran, and India—and more recently most of the Americas. But the peoples that moved into western Europe are the ones we are most interested in here. Almost all of them had some effect on English sooner or later, although the basic structure of our language was from the beginning Germanic. For English was founded on a succession of invasions of fifth century England by several tribes from the north coast of Europe—Jutes and Frisians, then Angles and Saxons—coming from territory that is now Holland, Northern Saxony, Schleswig-Holstein, and Denmark. The four tribes spoke closely related languages, all belonging to the subgroup that includes modern Dutch, Frisian, Flemish, and Platt-Deutsch—the so-called Low German group. Modern German and the languages of Scandinavia are slightly more distant relatives of English. And all these belong to the Germanic group, brother with the Greek, Latin, Slavic, Indic, and several other groups in the Indo-European family of languages. The kinship appears in many features of the languages, but it is probably easiest to see in vocabulary. Indo-European *leuk* (linguists indicate hypothetical forms by means of an asterisk) became English *light*, Greek *leukos*, Latin *lux*, Slavic (Bulgarian) *luca*, etc. Indo-European *reg* became English *rich*, Latin *rex*, Indic (Sanskrit) *raja*, etc.

Indo-European *nem or *nom became English *name,* Greek *onoma,* Latin *nomen,* Indic (Sanskrit) *nama,* etc.

The language that developed from these early northern European invasions of England had little to do with either the language of the British Celts who had been in the British Isles for a thousand years or so or the language of their Roman conquerors, who left after staying for about four centuries. It was almost entirely a Germanic language. In the influential West Saxon dialect, a woman speaks:

"Wulf, min Wulf, wena me þine seoce gedydon, þine seldcymas."

"Wolf, my Wolf, desires for you have made me sick, your rare visits."

A number of things about this sentence seem remarkable to us as speakers of Modern English. Many words show their kinship clearly, and "ween" and "did" and "coming" would make the remainder clear. *Seldcymas* ("seldom-comings") is a compound, and we are familiar with compound words in Modern English, although compounding would never again be as rich a source of new words as it was in Old English. The sentence order is not quite what we would expect in Modern English, even in poetry: "desires" and "rare visits" are both subjects of "made," and the Old English says, "Desires me for thee sick have made." But the most important difference is that much of the structural signaling is done by inflectional affixes—the kind of thing that you see in Latin *(amo, amas, amat),* in German *(liebe, liebst, liebt),* and even to some extent in Modern English *(book, books).* Old English uses a prefix in *ge–dydon* and suffixes *wen–a, þi–ne, seoc–e, dyd–on, cym–as.* That is one reason the sentence order can be freer, of course. We know by the inflection where things belong: *–cymas* must be nominative or accusative plural, *–dydon* must be preterite plural indicative, and so on. Along with a large portion of the vocabulary which has dropped out of the language by Modern English times, and a somewhat different sound system, this rather full inflectional system is the chief earmark of Old English. Inflection steadily decreased in elaboration and importance as English developed; Modern English, in fact, is almost uninflected. And Chaucer's English stands near the midpoint along that line of development.

3. History of English: through Middle English

Many of the developments that finally were to make Middle English quite a different language from Old English were apparent by 950, but we are given a clear dividing line by the events of 1066, when William the Norman brought his army ashore at Pevensey and went on to conquer England. This conquest did two kinds of things. Most important, it brought permanently into England a large and influential body of French speakers and their French culture, a group which took over the government and dominated the church, the army, and much of the cultivated life of the nation for well over two hundred years. Yet, the *absolute* domination of England by French speakers, and therefore by French, disappeared gradually, as Normans came to consider themselves Englishmen; and the old language, driven by the Conquest out of court, government, religion, warfare, began to be deliberately cultivated again by the ruling class. That introduces the second effect of the Norman Conquest, and a more controversial one. After the Conquest, English had become the principal property of the lower socioeconomic group for several centuries. When it emerged again as the sole national tongue, it had a very different look from the English spoken before 1066. It had absorbed more than 5,000 French words; it had lost all but a few of its old inflections (like the –*s* possessive, for example); and it had greatly altered the sound of many of its words. Perhaps the use of English solely by uneducated speakers speeded the changes that were occurring in English. Perhaps the use of a kind of pidgin English by Normans with their English herdsmen, craftsmen, and parish priests motivated the dropping of inflections. Perhaps many such factors, resulting from the collision of tongues, were responsible for the great changes in English over the two centuries after the Conquest—we do not know. But fifty years before Chaucer wrote, the new kind of English had become the officially established language in every facet of English life—including government and courts of law.

Of course, all that we have said so far about English has pretended that the language was a uniform product. Actually, in Old English times people spoke West Saxon or Kentish or Mercian or Northumbrian dialect, and in Middle English times they spoke Southern or Kentish or Midlands or Northern. What we call our "standard" language emerged later. On the other hand, every age of a language has its influential dialects; King Alfred's West Saxon was one, in the Old English period, and Chaucer's South-East Midlands was another, in Middle English times. In each case the dialect was important not because of any special virtue of its own, but because it was spoken by a group that was dominant in war, politics, and trade. It was just this sort of social dominance that made the London English in which Chaucer had the luck to be writing the basis for the modern Standard English which was to grow with the Renaissance.

4. *History of English: Modern English*

The beginning of the Renaissance in England—put it where you will between 1450 and 1500—marks the end of Middle English and the beginning of Modern English. Some characteristics of the language you and I speak appeared in later centuries: Shakespeare probably said "moother" and "tay" for "mother" and "tea." But most of the processes that make Modern English "modern" were finished by the close of the Renaissance. The most sweeping change was the Great Vowel Shift, during which the vowels we usually call "long" all shifted articulatory position, and shifted quite symmetrically, the fronter vowels going up and forward (say "bay" and then "bee" and feel your jaw going up and your tongue forward) and the back vowels up and back. What was produced was this sort of linguistic party game:

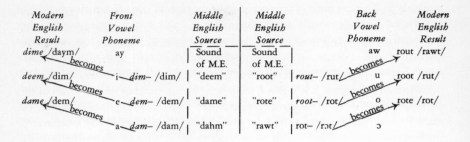

Modern English Result	Front Vowel Phoneme	Middle English Source	Middle English Source	Back Vowel Phoneme	Modern English Result
dime /daym/ → becomes	ay	Sound of M.E. "deem"	Sound of M.E. "root"	aw	rout /rawt/
deem /dim/ → becomes	i — dim- /dim/	"deem"	"root" — rout- /rut/ → becomes	u	root /rut/
dame /dem/ → becomes	e — dem- /dem/	"dame"	"rote" — root- /rot/ → becomes	o	rote /rot/
	a — dam- /dam/	"dahm"	"rawt" — rot- /rɔt/ → becomes	ɔ	

To put it another way, a Middle English word that would have sounded to us something like "hot" became *hate* during this period. So it was with the following pairs (giving first the approximate sound the M.E. word would have had for us, then the word that resulted from the Great Vowel Shift): "mane"/*mean*, "seen"/*sign*, "caught"/*coat*, "boat"/*boot*, "moose"/*mouse*. But before this change was well under way, the invention of printing and the vast changes which that produced had begun to crystallize English spelling. For this reason we inherit a writing system which really fits Chaucer's English better than ours. The Renaissance also saw the weakening of distinctions among unaccented vowels, a process that has now reached a point in English where words like "unsociable," though spelled as if they had four or more different vowels really have only two: /ənsošəbəl/. But in some ways the most dramatic change in the modern period of English was brought about by a Renaissance borrowing binge that brought 12,000 new words into the language, many from Latin and Greek. Not all of these borrowings became permanent, but those that did have had an enormous influence on the character of Modern English. And they serve as a reminder that vocabulary is one of the ways in which we can expect Chaucer's English to differ from ours.

5. *Chaucer's English: Vocabulary*

In addition to the stock of native English words, Chaucer had French borrowings of all kinds to draw on. These borrowings ranged from the simple (like "simple") to the recondite (like "chivachie"); they included Norman French ("*reward*") and Central French ("*guerd*on"); and some bore the marks of exotic travels before reaching France (like "almageste" and "Dulcarnon"). An important group of French borrowings reflected the difference between French and native English interests and pursuits—for example, the difference between native herdsmen and French cooks: *cu*, "cow," from Old English, but *beef* from Old French *boef*; *pig* from Old English, but *porc* from Old French, etc. Most were recently enough arrived in the language so that usage was divided about stress; almost all could be stressed in the French manner, on the final syllable, or according to the English pattern, on what native speakers took to be the root syllable (sometimes they were wrong).

French was not the only language to lend words to English. Among the stock available to Chaucer were words from Latin borrowed over the entire period of growth of English, words from Scandinavian, and words from some other European tongues. But despite all this foreign element, Chaucer had no trouble talking without using a single borrowed word: *A knyght ther was, and that a worthy man.* That expression seems quite natural and lucid to us today. As a matter of fact, Chaucer's familiar native words are like his exotic foreign words from one standpoint: neither group is the source of greatest trouble for the Modern English reader. It is not Chaucer's *chivachie* and *almageste* that make trouble for us as students of Middle English. It is his *coy* and *verray*—words whose face is familiar, but whose function in the language soon turns out to be a trap for the undiscriminating. For a complex pattern of semantic shifts has given us Modern English words whose meanings would have seemed ridiculous to Chaucer—*coy* meaning "coquettish," for example, where Chaucer would have used it to mean "meek" or "quiet." Often, as in the case of *coy,* Chaucer's meaning was closer to the etymological meaning—here Latin *quietus.* Below is a list of the most troublesome of these "misleading cognates," and a bit of memory work now will save many a twisted reading later.

Misleading Cognates (NOTE WELL: ALL OF THESE WORDS HAVE SEVERAL MEANINGS, ONLY THE MOST TROUBLESOME OF WHICH ARE LISTED BELOW. For example, M.E. *also* will not present a problem when it means "also," which is frequently; but it is important to remember that it will often mean "as.")

also = as; *also God my soule save,* "as God may save my soul"
agayn(s) = up to, in front of; *he was come agayns thilke pyrie,* "he came up to that pear tree"
anon = immediately; *I was of hir felaweshipe anon,* "I was immediately one of them"
aventure = chance; *what aventure hath gided the?,* "what chance has guided thee?"
bounte(e) = goodness; *Nature never formed so moche bounte wythoute mercy,* "Nature never formed so much goodness without mercy."
buxom = obedient; *hir housbonde sholde be buxom unto his wyf,* "her husband should be obedient to his wife"
cas = condition, chance; *neyther cas ne fortune hym deceyven,* "neither chance nor fortune deceives him"
che(e)re = bearing, expression; *this shal be my cheere,* "this shall be my expression"
corage = heart; *in noble corage oughte ben arest,* "in a noble heart there should be restraint"

9

coy = meek; *hir smyling was ful symple and coy,* "her smile was quite innocent and meek"

daliaunce = conversation; *unto no wight dooth he daliaunce,* "he makes conversation with no one"

daungerous = stand-offish; *if I be daungerous, God yeve me sorwe,* "if I hold back, God give me sorrow"

drede = doubt; *it is no drede,* "there is no doubt"

drenche(n) = drown; *he shulde drenche lord and lady,* "he would drown lord and lady"

fe(e)re = companion; *wel sit it a woful wight to han a drery feere,* "it well suits a woeful man to have a dreary companion"

forward = agreement; *I made forward erly for to ryse,* "I made an agreement to rise early"

fredam = generosity; *hir hand is ministre of fredam for almesse,* "her hand is minister of generosity for alms"

gentil = having the qualities associated with exalted birth; *Therefore sholden ye be gentil men,* "therefore you should be noble men"

governaunce = control, behavior; *nought knowynge of his false governaunce,* "knowing nothing of his deceitful behavior"

honeste(e) = decency; *for honestee no vileyns word spak he,* "for decency's sake he said nothing disgraceful"

kynde = nature; *agaynes kynde it were to lyven in thys wyse,* "it would be against nature to live this way"

lette(n) = hinder; *thou lettest oure disport,* "you're hindering our pleasure"

lust = pleasure; *of huntyng for the hare was al his lust,* "his great pleasure was hunting the hare"

nyce = foolish; *be no wyght so nyce to take a love oonly for chere,* "let no one be so foolish as to take a wife simply for her face"

quite(n) = repay; *ful wel koude I thee quite,* "I could easily repay thee"

richesse = nobility; *vyce may wel be heir to old richesse,* "vice may well be heir to former nobility"

sad = serious; *in the brest of hire virginitee ther was enclosed rype and sad corage,* "in the breast of her virginity was enclosed a mature and serious heart"

sely = good, innocent, poor; *algate this sely mayde is slayn, allas,* "still this poor, innocent maid is slain, alas"

skile = reason; *I can shewe hym swyche skiles,* "I can show him such reasons"

solempne = ceremonious, festive; *smale foules songen the moste solempne servise,* "little birds sang the most festive service"

spille(n) = destroy; *what joie hastow thyn owen folk to spille?,* "what joy hast thou to destroy thine own people?"

sterve(n) = die; *pitee were I shulde sterve,* "it would be a pity if I should die"

tho = then, those; *I was able to have lerned tho,* "I could have learned then," *thoo that hadde doon unkyndenesse,* "those that had been cruel" *trouthe* = faithfulness, pledge; *ye shul youre trouthe holden,* "you shall keep your word"

verray = true; *pleyn delit was verray felicitee parfit,* "simple pleasure was the true, perfect felicity"

wood = insane; *what sholde he studie and make hymselven wood?,* "why should he study and drive himself mad?"

worship = honor; *I besette my wyt to do hir worship,* "I put my mind to doing her honor"

wynne(n) = gain; *I am wont to preche for to wynne,* "I am accustomed to preach for gain"

yerne = eagerly; *myne handes and my tonge goon so yerne,* "my hands and tongue go so eagerly"

Rather on the other side from familiar words with strange meanings stand Chaucer's unfamiliar words, many of them the last vestiges of Old English forms that would die out in the Renaissance. Perhaps the most troublesome of this group are the strong verbs. As English speakers we are used to dealing with "swim, swam, swum"; but when we encounter *wat* or *hight* we have no clue that would send us to *witen* or *hoten.* The same bafflement is produced by contracted forms (*bit* for *biddeth*), by remnants of old inflections (*alderbest* for "best of all"), and, of course, by obsolete words (*fele* for "many"). A few of these obsolete or otherwise difficult forms survive in set expressions, like "I'd rather do it myself," where the Middle English *rathe* for "soon" can be made out. (Compare this with "I'd sooner die than do it.") Many more survive in dialect, like *mowe* and *sicker* in Scotland. Quite a number of these problems will be discussed next under morphology, but let us give a selected list here of strange forms that will be met often enough to deserve memorizing.

Obsolete or Difficult Forms (NOTE WELL: ALL OF THESE WORDS HAVE SEVERAL MEANINGS, ONLY THE MOST TROUBLESOME OF WHICH ARE LISTED BELOW. For example, M.E. *als* can mean "also," but it is probably most troublesome for the Modern English reader when it means "as.")

al = although; *al be that I knowe nat Love in deed,* "although it is true that I don't know of love from experience" (cf. Mod. E. "albeit")

als = as; *als evere moot I thryve,* "as I hope to thrive"

algate = anyway, still; *algate this sely mayde is slayn, allas,* "still this poor, innocent maid is slain, alas"

blyve = quickly; *goo now faste and hye the blyve,* "go fast now and hurry quickly"

brenne(n) = burn; *I made hym brenne his book,* "I made him burn his book"

breyde(n) = start, jump; *she of hir swough gan breyde,* "she started from her swoon"

clepe(n) = call; *Pan, that men clepe god of kynde,* "Pan, whom men call god of nature"

11

conne(n), konne(n) = know; *his lessoun, that he wende konne,* "his lesson, which he thought he knew"

fele = many; *with floures fele,* "with many a flower"

ferre = farther; *er I bere the moche ferre,* "before I bear thee much farther"

fonde(n) = try; *she wolde not fonde to holde no wyght in balaunce,* "she would not try to string a man along"

forthy = therefore; *forthy I is come,* "therefore I have come"

hap = chance; *shal I clepe hyt hap other grace?,* "shall I call it chance or luck?"

hende = able, gracious; *on a day this hende Nicholas fil with this yonge wyf to rage and pleye,* "one day this able Nicholas chanced to be playing and joking with this young wife"

hight(e) = called; *this Reve sat upon a ful good stot that highte Scot,* "this reeve sat on a very good horse called 'Scot' "

hye = haste; *by the hond in hye she took hym faste,* "by the hand in haste she took fast hold of him"

lyte = little; *in thy hed ful lyte is,* "very little is in thy head"

me(e)de = reward, bribe; *by no force ne by no meede he was nat able for to speede,* "he couldn't succeed by force or bribe"

mette(n) = dream; *me mette eek I was at a feeste,* "I dreamed also that I was at a feast"

mo(o)t = must; *and but I speke, I mot for sorwe deye,* "and unless I speak, I must die of sorrow"

mowe(n) = may; *we mowe swymme as in a barge,* "we may float as in a barge"

nadde (ne hadde) = had not; *nadde comfort ben of hire presence, I hadde be ded,* "if comfort had not been part of her, I would have died"

nere (ne were) = were not; *if it nere to long to heere,* "if it were not too long to listen to"

nis, nys (ne is) = is not; *in this world nys creature lyvynge* "there is not a creature living in this world"

no fors = no matter; *therof no fors,* "no matter about that"

nolde (ne wolde) = would not; *there was no dore that he nolde heve of harre,* "there was no door that he would not heave off its hinges"

no(o)t (ne wot) = know not; *I noot how men hym calle,* "I don't know his name"

nyste (ne wyste) = knew not; *I nyste never wher that I was,* "I knew not where I was"

or = ere, before; *or he sterve,* "before he dies"

paraunter = perhaps; *paraunter brod as a covercle,* "perhaps as a broad as a pot-cover"

rathe = soon; *other late or rathe,* "either late or soon" (cf. Mod. E. "I'd rather do it, I'd sooner do it")

shende(n) = injure; *n'apoplexie shente nat hir heed,* "nor did apoplexy injure her head"

12

siker = sure; *be thou siker,* "you may be sure"

sithen = then, afterwards; *to pieces do me drawe, and sithen honge,* "have me drawn to pieces and then hanged"

steven = voice; *he crew with blisful steven,* "he crowed with a happy voice"

stynte(n) = stop; *he stynte a while,* "he stopped a while"

sweven = dream; *this was my sweven,* "this was my dream"

swich = such; *swich fyn hath his estat real above,* "such an end hath his lofty royal state"

swynke(n) = work; *men that swynke,* "men that work"

swythe, swithe = swiftly; *this foul so swithe gan descende,* "this bird so swiftly did descend"

trowe(n) = believe; *it was almoost a spanne brood, I trowe,* "it was almost a span broad, I believe"

unnethe = hardly; *unnethe it sene was in his chere,* "it could hardly be seen in his face"

wisly = surely; *as wisly as I sey the,* "as surely as I saw thee"

wot = know (check *witen); nat wot I wel wher that I flete or synke,* "I do not know whether I float or sink"

wrie(n) = turn, cover; *men hem wrien with asshen pale,* "people cover them with pale ashes"

yfe(e)re = together; *she and alle hir folk in went yfeere,* "she and all her people went in together"

ywis = certainly; *that ye han seyd is right ynough, ywis,* "what you have told is enough certainly"

6. *Chaucer's English: Morphology*

When we use the term *grammar* in this booklet, we will mean "the way language works, its system," and not "correct usage" or "rules for writing"—just in case you have been using the term to include those. Grammar can be divided into *morphology*—the patterns *within words* that signal how the words will work, like the inflections that we spoke of earlier—and syntax—the patterns within the sentence that show how its parts work—which we often call "word order." Chaucer's grammar is essentially that of Modern English, and the only way to make it seem complicated is to discuss it from the standpoint of Old English, or to pretend that none of us speak Modern English. To tell the truth, Chaucer's morphology—the pattern of grammatical signals within his words—will be very smooth going for any speaker of Modern English who keeps in mind some thirteen "conversion factors," or principal points of difference between the grammar of Chaucer's English and the grammar of our own.

Nouns:

(1) Chaucer could make possessives of some kinds of nouns without using an ending:

in hope to stonden in his lady grace, "in hopes of winning his lady's favor"

13

he wolde lede algate hys fader carte, "he still wanted to drive his father's chariot"

(2) Chaucer never marks his possessives with an apostrophe:
have ye no mannes herte?, "haven't you a man's heart?"

Adjectives:

Chaucer used three kinds of adjectives that sometimes confuse modern readers.

(3) 1) *aller* (or *alder*) for "of all"—*he was oure aller cok,* "he was rooster for us all"

(4) 2) *lenger, strenger,* etc., for "longer," "stronger," etc.—*what shuld I make lenger tale?,* "why should I make a longer list?"

(5) 3) a few unusual comparatives, like *werre,* "worse," and *bet,* "better"—*I shulde have pleyed the bet at ches,* "I should have played chess better"

Pronouns:

Aside from strong verbs, pronouns are the most ticklish area of Chaucer's grammar.

(6) 1) *ich* appears as well as *I* for "I."

(7) 2) *his* may mean "its" as well as "his"; Chaucer does not use "its."

(8) 3) *hire* (or *here*) and *hem* were Chaucer's only forms for "their" and "them."

(9) 4) *these* and *thise* were used interchangeably.

Verbs:

(10) 1) Chaucer sometimes used forms for plural, infinitive, and past participle which end in *–en.* The *–en* forms occasionally help in a reading (*that* in *that slepen al the nyght with open ye,* for example, must have a plural antecedent), but the forms in *–e* and *–en* vary freely: *which they weren* (pl.) *... and eek in what array that they were* (pl.) *inne,* or *His lord wel koude he plesen* (infin.) *subtilly/ To yeve* (infin.) *and lene* (infin.) *hym of his owene good.*

(11) 2) Some verb forms, when inflected, result in a combination of a final *–d* or *–t* or *–th* with an ending in *–eth* (sitteth; biddeth). This result is frequently contracted to leave nothing but *–t: sit, bit,* (*it sit wel to be so,* "it sitteth well to be so," i.e., "it is fitting that it is so"). These puzzling forms will probably appear in your glossary.

(12) 3) Chaucer occasionally uses *–y* to mark the past participle: *ysungen,* "sung."

(13) 4) Middle English *gan* is often an auxiliary like Modern English "did": *gan to praise,* "praised," i.e., "did praise," contrasted with *gan syngen,* "began to sing."

7. *Chaucer's English: Syntax*

The other part of the grammar of Chaucer's English is somewhat more troublesome to us—his syntax, or word order. It is troublesome partly because word order is the most crucial technique of grammatical signaling in Modern English, and anything unfamiliar in this area makes us uneasy. The other troublesome side to Chaucer's syntax is that it is almost impossible to codify briefly. Luckily, the part of it that does not seem natural to you as a speaker of Modern English will seem natural to you as a reader of Middle English before long, for the "logic" of word order is very persuasive to anyone who sets aside his preconceptions and turns on his sensitivity. It will be useful as you learn to keep in mind a few syntactical "conversion factors."

Nouns:
- **(1)** 1) Chaucer avoided one possessive construction that we accept and said *he was the king Priamus sone of Troye* for "he was King Priam of Troy's son."
- **(2)** 2) Even more freely than we, Chaucer used as nouns some words that look like adjectives: *Alwey the nye slye maketh the ferre leeve to be looth,* "A sly one nearby always makes a far loved one despised."

Pronouns:

The use Chaucer makes of *that* poses several problems for the Modern English reader:
- **(3)** 1) If you are translating, you will sometimes simply omit it: *when that April,* "when April."
- **(4)** 2) Sometimes *that* enters into a straightforward equivalent of an inverted modern construction: *Ther nas bailiff . . . that he ne knew his sleighte,* "There was no bailiff whose tricks he didn't know."
- **(5)** 3) Quite often *that* equals Modern English "what": *He kepte that he wan in pestilence,* "He kept what he got during the plague." This is exactly parallel to Chaucer's use of *ther: Ther as this lord was kepere of the celle,* "Where this lord ruled the priory."

Verbs:
- **(6)** Chaucer often uses an impersonal construction where Modern English would introduce a personal subject: *Thee nedeth nat the galle of noon hyene,* (i.e., "it needs you not the gall of a hyena," for Modern English "you don't need . . .")

Adverbs:
- **(7)** 1) In separable verbs (like "look up" in "he looked up the number"), Chaucer tended to keep the verb and adverb together: *an heyre clowt to wrap in me,* "a hair-cloth to wrap myself in."
- **(8)** 2) Several uses of *as* have Modern English equivalents without "as": *ye sholden sterve as yerne,* "you would die quickly"; *as wolde God,* "would to God"; (notice the parallel use of *also—also God youre soule blesse* —and of *ther—ther God his bones corse*).

15

(9)   Finally, Chaucer quite often changed his syntax in midstream, in a way that we do in conversation, but avoid in writing: *The noise up ros, whan it was first aspied thorugh al the town, and generally was spoken, that Calkas traitour fled was an allied with hem of Grece, and kasten to be wroken. . . .* , "The noise rose up when it was first found out through all the town and generally spoken that Calcas was fled as a traitor and allied with those of Greece, and [the towns-people] decided to be avenged. . . ."

THE SOUNDS OF CHAUCER'S ENGLISH

PHONOLOGY

1. *Introduction*

From about a hundred years after Chaucer's death until the middle of the nineteenth century, it was generally thought that Chaucer's poetry, though excellent in conception, was somewhat primitive in its organization of sound into meter, rhyme, and so on. The great Neoclassical poet Dryden, though he recognized clearly Chaucer's greatness, found his meters remarkably uneven; according to Dryden, Chaucer wrote in the "infancy" of the language; naturally, therefore, his verses were irregular. Yet "there is the rude sweetness of a Scotch tune in it, which is natural and pleasing, though not perfect." In sum, Chaucer is "a rough diamond, and must first be polished ere he shines."

Even at that time, however, some scholars suspected that Chaucer's lines sounded much more regular and sweet to the fourteenth century ear than to the eighteenth. What they suspected we now know to be true. Dryden could not hear Chaucer's verse properly because he could not pronounce it as Chaucer did. In the middle of the last century, there occurred one of the great triumphs of systematic scholarship. The sound system (phonology) of Middle English was painstakingly recovered. And it became clear that Chaucer was not a rough diamond at all—though he was by no means as regular a metrist as Dryden was —but a poet with one of the finest ears for the music of speech that English literature has to boast of, in his or in any other time.

Obviously, this obsolete sound system was not recovered through the sudden appearance of a living speaker of fourteenth century London English. What happened was that the language was reconstructed sound by sound, from a careful study of written records. This tremendous feat took some time, and scholars are still refining their earlier conclusions, but today the sounds of by far the largest number of Chaucer's consonants, consonant clusters, and vowels have been reconstructed beyond any reasonable doubt. These reconstructions must always be more or less approximate, but they are very far from guesswork.

What this booklet hopes to teach, therefore, is an approximate pronunciation of Chaucer's dialect—all we are ever likely to have, and a good deal better than nothing. But in fairness to the reconstruction, we should point out that its "approximateness" is ascribable partly to a range of legitimate pronunciations in the original dialect so obviously wide as to present us with no sure single standard. And there is almost no doubt that this pronunciation of Chaucer's English would have been understood in the London of his time—as, say, a

German who has studied English in school can be understood in London now, or a BBC commentator can be understood in America.

It is fair to ask how we know what the language sounded like. Students of the phonology of tongues that are no longer spoken obviously have only written records to work from. But it is possible to draw surprisingly firm conclusions from written records alone, provided there are enough of them. The primary forms of evidence are such things as:

a. Sounds used consistently to form rhymes (*you* and *through* are rhymes in Modern English, but in Middle English they are never rhymed);

b. Sounds used consistently to form alliterative patterns (*gnaw* and *now* have the same initial sound in Modern English, but in Middle English alliterative verse *gnaw* has the same initial sound as *gate, God,* etc.);

c. Remarks made by writers of the language upon its peculiarities, or attempts by writers of other languages to represent its sounds in terms of their own spelling systems;

d. Spelling systems used consistently either by grammarians or by unskilled writers in a conscious effort to represent the sounds of the language accurately. (Thus *nite* and *thoro* and *thru* and *laff* are "simplified" or modern spellings supposed to represent the "real" modern sounds of these words; *night* and *thorough* and *through* and *laugh,* like *gnaw* and *know,* are spellings left over from the Middle English period, when the words sounded different.) In Chaucer's epoch particularly—but to a lesser degree in the subsequent two centuries as well—the relation between spelling and sound was much closer and freer than it is in our own time. First, there was neither a single preeminent dialect nor a single accepted spelling system. For though in each dialect there were customary "literary" ways of representing some sounds, such spelling systems were far from universally known; and many people, especially the unprofessional writers, essentially had to try to transcribe what they spoke. Thus we have a great deal of "badly" spelled—and phonologically speaking very useful—material from this epoch to work from.

There are other less obvious ways of working back to an obsolete phonological system. This reconstruction is a difficult but not impossible task, when there are enough written records. In the case of London English in Chaucer's time, a huge carefully accumulated and sifted mass of such data allows us to feel reasonably certain that we know how the vowels and consonants of that language sounded. At present we have no analytical tool that can help us to know what its intonation patterns (pitch, pause, stress, etc.) were; thus its melody is lost. On the other hand, Chaucer's versification itself—dependent partly on pause and stress patterns—can tell us something even about this, as long as we are dealing with verse.

18

2. Sounds and Spellings

As it happens, there was a remarkable freeze of English spelling not long after Chaucer's day, perhaps partly because of the invention of printing. Thus our standard way of spelling imitates not the contemporary sounds of the language so much as the older ones preserved through a written tradition. But that written tradition was itself once an effort to represent actual speech—the speech of Chaucer's time or shortly after. We are lucky, therefore, in that most of the spellings of Chaucer's words are familiar to us as the spellings of our own words; our luck is perhaps a little dubious in that these spellings are more useful to us in pronouncing Chaucer's words than in pronouncing our own. In studying Middle English we have only a few "new" (i.e., obsolete) sounds to learn to make, and the way a word is spelled is a pretty good clue to the way it is pronounced. In some cases spellings of familiar words have changed in the intervening time (*weder/weather; fadre/father; bridde/bird; nye/nigh*). Such cases present little difficulty if we pronounce the Middle English phonemes in the order in which the written language represents them (e.g., *d* instead of *th* in *fadre, ri* instead of *ir* in *bridde,* etc.). But most words were spelled pretty much then as now, and our basic job is to learn to repronounce the sounds still represented in our written but not in our spoken tongue. (Many current nonstandard dialect forms, on the other hand, frequently represent Middle English or later pronunciations. To take just one example, the dialect familiar to most of us only as Hollywood Western is largely eighteenth century English: "How do ye?" became "Howdy?"; "creature" became "critter.") Because of the Great Vowel Shift (see p. 7 above) things are a little more complicated with the vowels than with the consonants.

3. Consonants

We may say with reasonable security that with a very few exceptions, consonant sounds in Chaucer's speech not only are very like our own but also are represented quite consistently by the letters of his written language. Every consonantal letter in Chaucer's text has some phonetic value, except for *g* before *n* in recent French borrowings such as *digne,* and initial *h* (hotel, hogges, his, hadde) in most positions; and aside from these "silent" consonants and a few other sounds (those represented by *gh* and *r,* and perhaps also those represented by double consonants such as *ll, dd, tt*), all we need to do to handle Chaucer's consonantal letters reasonably well is to pronounce *all* of them. Thus the *g* in *gnaw,* the *k* in *know,* the *wr* in *wreak,* the *sw* in *answer* all represent sounds actually produced in Middle English, and those sounds are familiar to us in Modern English words: *g* as in *gut, k* as in *kin, wr* approximately as in *worry, sw* as in *sweat.* These few differences, and the even fewer ones that present more of a problem, we will come to later in detail in conjunction with the recording.

4. Vowels

Analysis of rhymes shows clearly that almost all our "short" vowels (see

19

record script, *Vowels, General Note*), as in modern *bit* (contrast to modern *bite*), *bed* (contrast to *bead*), *top* (contrast to *toper*) have changed very little since Chaucer's time, *when we preserve those short vowels in stressed syllables:* our *bit* is very little different from Chaucer's *bit;* our *bet* is not greatly different from his *bet.* The most important change in the pronunciation of short vowels in English is the general leveling of almost all of them, when they occur in unstressed syllables, to a neutral "uh" sound (as in our previous example, *unsociable*), usually called the neutral vowel, and assigned the phonetic symbol ə. If in reading Chaucer we simply pronounce all short vowels as if stressed— with the single but important exception of final, vestigial *–e* in such words as *sone, bridde, handes,* which apparently had already become the neutral vowel— we will be able to reconstitute the short vowels of Chaucer's language fairly well. Our "long" vowels, on the other hand, have undergone very considerable changes: some of them have changed once; others have changed twice or even three times in the six centuries that cut us off from Chaucer. All the long vowels that once were single sounds (i.e., like most of the vowels of modern Italian) have become slightly or markedly diphthongized—or have become short. The vowels in *root, good,* and *blood,* separated in Modern English, were the same in Middle English—as their spelling indicated—and were pronounced approximately like the *o* in modern *rode* or *hoe,* but without the diphthong u-glide that some careful listeners can hear clearly.

These changes in the long vowels are the most difficult obstacles we face in learning to pronounce Chaucer's dialect well. They are in no sense impossible to master, yet without their mastery we cannot get full value from Chaucer's language—for he intended that language to be read aloud, and he intended its sound to amplify and to extend its sense.

5. *Meter*

The recovery of Chaucer's phonology showed immediately that the meter of his poetry was probably considerably different from what Dryden thought. Critically important here were syllabification, accentuation, and elision.

Because during Chaucer's time, as we have seen, English was in the middle of its transition from a highly inflected language (Old English) to one depending almost entirely on word order and function words (Modern English), remnants of the old inflectional system are still evident in Southeast Midland. These remnants, though few, were evidently pronounced, though during Chaucer's lifetime Londoners probably began to elide, to slur, or even to drop some of them completely in speech. We should conceive of these changes as gradual. By 1370, for example, the younger generation might have ceased pronouncing final *–e* in many words while the older generation still pronounced it invariably. We know with certainty only that the change occurred during Chaucer's lifetime, and that a hundred years after his death Londoners evidently had lost even the option of pronouncing these inflectional remnants. But by and large, during Chaucer's lifetime all of them apparently could be pronounced in formal speech

—and poetry is a distinctly formal kind of language. Thus *wordes* (words) had two syllables; *large* had two syllables; *wente* had two; and so on. Once we understood that in effect the final *-e, -es,* and *-en* were not unpronounced scribal peculiarities—that syllables generally represented in written Middle English spelling are represented because they can be or are pronounced—our whole attitude toward Chaucer's meter had to change.

One aspect of this phonological situation was particularly useful to Chaucer as a metrist—and bewildering to his successors. Chaucer had available to him metrically variant forms for many if not for most of the words in his language. *Boke* could have one syllable or two; so could *bokes*. *Lyth* and *lyeth* were both legitimate forms of the same word. Chaucer could say "she was *named*" in at least four ways: she was *cleped,* she was *clept,* she was *ycleped,* she was *yclept.* And so on. His freedom in choosing among these forms is not absolute, to be sure—far from it—but it is very great, and affords him tremendous flexibility as a metrist.

In this respect, too, the patterns of elision in Chaucer's language are of considerable importance. Elision in Chaucer is subject to a certain number of definite if flexible rules; but our discussion need not be highly technical. Chaucer elides *-e* regularly though not invariably before words beginning with a vowel or with *h,* as in

> So graunte(e) him soon(e) out of this world to pace. . . .

(In some words, such as *were, hire, youre, there, bifore, made,* the *-e* is never pronounced, except when the words are used as rhyme.) But Chaucer also drops *e* with fair regularity in unaccented syllables, if he must do so in order to prevent two unstressed syllables from following a stressed one:

> In felaw(e)ship(e), and pilgrim(e)s were they alle.

He also frequently appears to unite *the* to following vowels, or to words with initial *h:*

> Purs is th(e) ercedeknes hell(e), seyd(e) he.
> And al th'honour that men may don yow have. . . .
> In alle th(e) ordres four(e) is noon that kan. . . .

In general, your own ear for the basic metrical pattern is a more practical guide than a set of intricate rules could be, provided that you remember throughout that Chaucer is not a mechanical poet running forever in iambs, and that a metrically slavish rendering of his verse will destroy much of its beauty. There is simply no way by which we can make the lines describing the Hunting Monk's love of harness bells fall into regular iambic pentameter—and no value in even trying:

21

And whan he rood, men myght(e) his brydel heere
Gynglen in a whystlyng(e) wynd als cleere
And eek as loud(e) as dooth the chapel belle.

It was our earlier ignorance of these aspects of Chaucer's language that led to Dryden's judgment that Chaucer was a rough poet. The following "unequal" lines from the General Prologue of the *Canterbury Tales* Dryden represents (in somewhat modernized spelling) thus:

Or else he mote tellen his tale untrue	(10 syllables)
Or feine things or find words new	(7 syllables)

But they have a very different metrical structure once it is realized that the sounds represented in the Middle English texts but eliminated later as "unnecessary" would have resulted in quite different sounding lines of 10 syllables each:

Or ellis he moot tell(e) his tal(e) untrewe	(13 syllables, of which two elided and one at end)
Or feyne thyng, or fynde wordes newe	(11 syllables, of which one forms the feminine ending)

The impact on the syllabification and accentuation of Chaucer's English of the many borrowings from Norman French during the medieval period also came under study, and it became clear that the whole class of nouns such as *nacioun, visioun,* etc., had one syllable more then than they do now (na–ci–oun, vi–si–oun)—and could be accented according to the French rule, on the *last* syllable, rather than according to the standard English rule (accentuation on the first or root syllable). Similarly, in Chaucer's time French words like *citee* could be accented after the English rule, on the root syllable, or after the French rule, on the last; their accent was in transition. Thus the lines, "In divers ways and in diverse figures," in which it is clear that Chaucer intended to accent *divers* on the first syllable and *diverse* on the second, and "In no citee ne in no village," in which it is highly probable that both *citee* and *village* are accented on the second syllable and that each has three syllables. Once, therefore, Chaucer's different and much more flexible syllabification and accentuation system and his continuous and quite natural recourse to elision are understood, his "unpolished" numbers are suddenly discovered to need not anyone's polishing—though, to be sure, he is not as regular as is Dryden or Pope.

At this stage, direct practice of Chaucer's phonology in conjunction with the record will take you furthest fastest. There follow three series of nonsense exercises designed to help you learn the major phonological differences between the Middle English of Chaucer's dialect and Modern English. Each exercise focuses on a single phonological difference; except for these differences, modern pronunciation is probably very close to that of Middle English and the modern pronunciation is a safe guide. The exercises focus first on consonants, then on short vowels, then on long vowels, as they appear in reasonably normal Middle English words and sentence structures. This method of training has real advantages but one disadvantage: although the focus of each nonsense exercise is on only one phonological difference, other phonological differences will appear. Do not worry about mastering everything immediately: do your best, but concentrate on the specific sound being exemplified. You can always try again.

One general caution: don't fall into the habit of using the entire sound system of a language other than English simply because you know it well and it sounds foreign. *Don't* use a French pronunciation in words such as *engendren,* or a German pronunciation in words such as *sterre,* etc. The differences detailed in the following pages are the *only* significant sound differences between Chaucer's dialect of Middle English and Modern English, as far as we know.

While the record is playing, read the pamphlet as you listen to the instructor's voice. *Do not try to read the notes* on each sound while you are actually recording—read them before or after. The actual record script is on the left-hand side of the page. After the instructor has pronounced the Middle English sound, the exemplary words, and the nonsense sentence containing these words, read the sequence aloud, either to a classmate or into a tape recorder microphone. Then wait for the next sequence. At the end rewind the tape, listen again to the instructor's voice on the record, followed by your own, and compare. You may then either repeat the drill or go on to the next sequence. In one way or another you should listen to and practice the recording of "The Sounds of Chaucer's English" at least twice before going on to the selections from Chaucer's poetry. *Above all,* remember that, by and large, Middle English spelling habits are direct efforts to represent actual sounds, and though far from consistent (in part because pronunciation itself is not consistent) these spelling habits are your best immediate guide to Middle English pronunciation, once you have learned a few simple rules.

For the convenience of those who already have or who wish to have a fair command of the system of phonetic *symbols* commonly used to describe the vowels of Middle English and their differences from Modern English, we provide at the end of this Introduction a short table of phonological equivalents. While study of this table may be useful, it is not necessary for one's acquiring a reasonable ability to read Chaucer aloud.

TABLE OF VOWEL EQUIVALENTS

Modern English
If the vowel of
the Modern English
word sounds like:

Middle English (London, 14th century)

... the vowel in Middle English sounds like:

Vowel	Word	Vowel	Word	Usual M.E. spelling	As in	Phonetic symbol	Older phonetic symbol
a	in man	o	in stop	a	*man*	a	
a	in name	a	in father	a, aa	*name*	a:	ā
au	in cause	ow	in cow	au, aw	*cause*	au	
i	in this	i	in this	i, y	*this*	ɪ	ī
i(y)	in sly	ee	in beet	i, y	*slye*	i:	ī
e	in met	e	in bet	e	*mette*	ɛ	e
e, ee	in sweet	a	in mate (no glide)	e, ee	*swete*	e:	ē·
ea	in heath	e	in there	e, ee	*heeth*	ɛ:	ę̄
age ("silent" e)		a	in sofa	e	*age*	ə	
ay	in day	e	in there	ai, ay			
		+y	in easy	ei, ey	*day*	ɛi	ę̄i
ew	in few	e	in bet			ɛu	ēu
		+w	in few	ew	*fewe*		
ew	in new	ew	in new	ew, uw	*newe*	iu	
o	in dog	o	in *Brit.* hot	o	*dogge*	ɔ	o
oo	in fool, blood, hood	o	in vote (no glide)	o, oo	*blood*	o:	ō·
o	in rode	aw	in bawdy (no glide)	o, oo	*rood*	ɔ:	ǭ
ow	in grow	ow	in grow	ow	*growen*	ou	ou·
ou	in fought	o	in *Brit.* hot				
		+w	in few	ow, ou	*foughten*	ɔu	ǭu
o	in love	u	in put	u, o	*love*	ʊ	u
ou	in loud	u	in rule	ou, ow	*loud*	u:	ū
u	in nature, virtue	u	in *Fr.* tu	u	*nature*	y:	ü

THE SOUNDS OF CHAUCER'S ENGLISH

RECORD SCRIPT AND NOTES

RECORD SCRIPT

NOTES

As noted before, our knowledge of the phonology of Chaucer's dialect is far from guesswork. See the preceding section of this booklet.

This is what Chaucer's language probably sounded like:

At the same time, any attempt to reconstruct artificially a tongue no longer spoken is bound to run into some theoretical problems; and any attempt to speak such a tongue is bound to run into practical problems as well. A careful listener will hear occasional deviations in this recording from the phonetic norms established in the record script; he will also hear a few clear failures in accentuation, syllabification, and elision. Even if everything were known about Chaucer's dialect (and though much is known, not everything is), a modern would find some difficulty in speaking it with absolute consistency. This recording does not try to teach a totally accurate 14th century London dialect; that cannot be done. It does try to teach a version of that dialect sufficiently accurate to be serviceable to those who wish an understanding of its poetry.

> Ye knowe ek that in forme of
>   speche is chaunge
> Withinne a thousand yeer, and
>   wordes tho
> That hadden pris, now wonder nyce
>   and straunge
> Us thinketh hem, and yet thei spake
>   hem so
> And speede as wel in love as men
>   now do;
> Ek for to wynnen love in sondry ages
> In sondry londes, sondry ben usages.

Troilus & Criseyde, II, 11. 22 ff.

Some of the differences between this and Modern English are in vocabulary.

Some are in syntax. But the largest changes are phonological. Most consonants are pronounced as they are now, but some consonants not now pronounced were pronounced then: *Ye knowe.* R is slightly trilled, and final *–e* is pronounced except where it needs to be elided to make the metrical pattern clearer: *in forme of speche is chaunge.* Some vowels were simple sounds then that now are diphthongs: *Withinne a thousand yeer.* Virtually all vowel sounds were different from their modern equivalents and sound a bit "rounder," like the vowels of modern Spanish or Italian: *And wordes tho, That hadden pris, now wonder nyce and straunge, Us thinketh hem, and yet thei spake hem so....*

Note that the *k* is sounded.

Note the *r* in *forme,* and elision of the final *–e* of *forme* and of *speche.* Note also that the preservation of the final *–e* of *chaunge* and of similar words gives the characteristic softness of the feminine ending to most of Chaucer's lines.

I. Consonants

General note: Consonant changes have been fairly numerous since Chaucer's time, but it is not difficult to work from our current literate spellings back to M.E. (Middle English) pronunciation. Generally the notes below concentrate on M.E.—Mod. E. (Modern English) differences and do not try to reflect fluctuations in usage in between except insofar as these may be useful in establishing Chaucer's use. Language does not change in a completely uniform and linear manner; some apparently widespread developments in our own language in the centuries separating us from Chaucer have since been reversed: e.g., *thousands, handful, grandmother* all lost their *d*'s and then had them largely reinstated (though colloquial Mod.E. often ignores the *d*); the same thing happened with the *b* in some words such as *nimbly,* the *r* in *first* and *burst,* and the *w* in *towards* and *leeward* (still pronounced by old salts as if spelled *loo-ard*), etc. It is impossible—and unimportant for our present purposes—to note all such changes and dialect tendencies in this guide.

Note also that we have omitted to deal with differences adequately represented by the differences in spelling between M.E. and Mod. E. Thus, in Chaucer's language we read *fader, moder, wieder,* etc., instead of *father, mother, weather.* The *d* was replaced by *th* after Chaucer's death. Chaucer's spelling reflects his pronunciation: all the reader need do is to read the word spelled by Chaucer.

1.a. *lk:* walk, stalk, talk
They walken, he stalketh, she talketh

1.b. *lf:* half, calf, wolf
Half a calf is bet than half a wolf

Since Chaucer's time the *l* of such consonant clusters has become silent generally between back vowels such as *a* (called *back* because they are articulated at the back of the mouth) and labial (p, b, f, v, m, w) or velar (g, k, ŋ) consonants (called *labial* or *velar* depending on whether the points of articulation are the lips or the soft palate).

2.a. *kn:* knave, knobbe, knowen
Knave, knoweth that I shal thy knobbes knokken till they aken.

The *k* and *g* of initial *kn* and *gn* clusters were virtually extinct in English as of the 16th C.; they survive only in such recent imports as *gnu*—and even here not in most dictionary guides—and *Knesset.*

2.b. *gn:* gnawen, gnarled, gnof, gnatte
A! Gnarled gnof, go gnawen at thy gnattes!

To make the sounds: a. say *canal,* then cut off the last syllable; b. say *ignore,* then cut off the *i* and the *ore.*

2.c. I nam nat digne to dinen here.

Medial *kn* as in *reknen* (we call a sound *medial* when it occurs in the middle of a word) is also sounded as above; so is medial *gn* where it (very rarely) occurs in words of Old English origin. In words of recent French origin, however, medial *gn* is pronounced *n*. Most cases of medial *gn* in Chaucer are of this latter class: *digne, signe, resigne,* etc. As a working rule, adopt the *n* pronunciation whenever you see medial *gn*.

3. *wh:* who, whynen, white, whale (hw)
Who whyneth so of whiche white whales?

Wh is also spelled *hw* in many M.E. texts. The *h* of this cluster began to disappear in some words such as *which, while,* in the 17th C., although it still remains in some dialects. In M.E. the *h* seems to have been articulated.

4. *ng:* thyng, syngen, strenge (ŋg)
He gooth syngyng of the strenges on his thynges.

Shortly after Chaucer's time—and even perhaps during it in the case of the participial ending *ing*—this sound became effectively the one we now pronounce twice in *ringing*. General opinion is, however, that the *g* of this cluster was still pronounced in Chaucer's verse, although it vanished completely by the 17th C. Note that the *n* of the cluster is the *n* of modern *sing*, not that of modern *sin*.

5. *r:* revelour, roten, ripe
This worthy revelour was roten er that he was ripe.

General opinion is that the *r* of Chaucer's speech was still trilled, or "flapped," though an untrilled variant may already have entered the language to form the ancestor of our modern untrilled *r*. It is generally thought that *r* began to be untrilled in the 16th C. The sound is made by air passing between the tongue (whose tip acts almost like a reed) and the front or hard palate. To make the sound: hold the edges of the mid portion of the tongue against the roof of the mouth, depressing the center channel of the tongue and keeping the tip relaxed but curled up toward the back of the front top teeth. Say *r* and blow. Relax and blow harder—exaggerate in order to hear the sound properly.

6.   *wr:* writen, wrecches, wreken, wronges
The wrecches writen that they wreken hem of wronges.

The *w* of this cluster is no longer pronounced (*wreck* and *ring* have the same initial sound). It is difficult to pronounce unless the *r* is strongly flapped. To make the sound: say *answer,* but pronounce the *w* and flap the *r.* Now say the second syllable only.

7.a.   *gh:* sight, fighten, knight (ç)
What a sight to seen thise dronkene knightes fighten!

This sound has been obsolete in standard London pronunciation since the 15th C. The sound represented by *gh* was very common in O.E. and M.E. and is preserved in our spelling of many words. In Chaucer its usual spelling is *gh,* as here, but it can be spelled merely as *h: thoght* or *thoht.* Modern spelling is a safe guide: if the cluster *gh* appears in the Mod.E. form of a M.E. word, the M.E. sound of that cluster is as here. The only exception is *delight,* which did not have *gh* in M.E. To make the sound: say the *h* of *hire,* but very forcefully. Or start to say *k* as in *leaky,* but make a scrape instead of a stop.

7.b. *gh:* laughen, saugh, foghten, thoughten (χ)
How we laughten what that we thoughten that they foughten for oon draught of wyn.

This sound has a history almost identical to that of the sound described above. Where final, as in *laugh* and *rough, gh* frequently changed to *f* (*laughter/lafter*) up to the 18th C., when it disappeared altogether (as it has in *fought, thought*) except in a few words, e.g., *laugh, enough, dwarf, rough.*

Again, modern spelling is a guide to M.E. pronunciation: even if the *g* is omitted from the M.E. word (thoghten /thohten), its presence in the Mod.E. form indicates the velar spirant in M.E.

To make the sound: say *lock* very forcefully, but don't "stop" the *k*, so that you are articulating something like an *h* at the same point in the mouth and with full breath.

8.a. *th:* either, other, brother (ð)
And either hateth other, leeve brother.

8.b. *th:* thin, this, sooth, the (θ)
The sooth is this, though loath I tell hit thee.

This is the "voiced" *th* of modern *their,* as opposed to the voiceless *th* of modern *thick* (if you put your fingers on your adam's apple and say the *th* of *their* you will feel a vibration, or *voicing;* you will not feel it if you say the *th* of *thick*). *Th* is invariably voiced in M.E. when it occurs between vowels, within a single word. When not between words, *th* is regularly unvoiced.

8.c. *s:* thise, glose, suffisen (z)
Thise gloses the suffisen, comparisouns ben odious.

The same situation pertains with respect to *s* as with respect to *th:* voiced when between vowels in the same word; voiceless when not.

8.d. *s:* this, was, is, sely (s)
This is a sely sight, how that the cherles ers is scorched.

8.e. *f:* fayre, captif, lif, strif (f)
She kepte hir lif, this fayre captif of strif.

8.f. *v:* captives, lives, wives, striven (v)
Until hir lives ende, thise captives striven to ben wives.

As with *th* and *s, f* when between vowels in the same word is voiced—which means that within the English spelling system it is usually changed to *v,* there being no difference between the two consonants in articulation except the matter of voicing.

30

9.   *gg:* juggen, hegge, brigge (d_3)
Whan hegges semen brigges,
than juggement is wood.

M.E. had but one cluster, *gg,* to represent two sounds: those represented respectively in Mod.E. *judge* and *jugged.* Thus in M.E. *hegge* and *begge* look as if they ought to rhyme. They do not, either in Mod.E. or in M.E. The distinction is clearer in Mod.E. spelling: *hedge* and *beg.* Modern pronunciation is the safest guide: words pronounced with *dg* in Mod.E. were so pronounced in M.E.; words pronounced with *g* in Mod.E. were so pronounced in M.E.

10. *h:* he, hath, historial, honour,
      hasardrie
He hath historial bookes of honour and hasardrie.

In M.E. words of recent French origin such as *hasard, hautein, hauberk, hostage, hosteleria,* the initial *h* is never pronounced and is sometimes not even spelled (thus Chaucer uses *storial* for *historial* and *spitel* for *hospital*).

The situation with initial *h* in other words is fairly ambiguous. In the personal pronouns *he, him, hire, hem,* etc., the *h* appears to have been dropped fairly readily when not in a stressed situation. But in a line like *"And in his armes he hem alle uphente"* (*Knight's Tale,* l. 957) it seems highly unlikely that *h* was uniformly dropped from all the pronouns. Nevertheless, in other clearly stressed contexts, the use of the variant forms *myn, thyn, an* (compare *myn herte* to *my lady* or to *my deere herte*) indicates that in almost all classes of words initial *h* was very weak: *myn housbonde, an houre, an hogges toord, an howve, an hewe, an huge reyn, thyn hestes, an heigh matiere.* We must conclude that initial *h* was pronounced forcefully only for special emphasis.

11. *ss, kk, pp, gg,* etc.: thikke, bittre, dogge lippe
This bittre dogge kisseth hir thikke thombe with his lippes and waggeth his dokked tayle.

As far as we can judge, doubled consonants in M.E. probably were an attempt to represent orthographically a sound of somewhat longer duration than did their single equivalents. Doubled consonants apparently served the purpose of contrasting rhythmically with the short vowels preceding them (a long vowel is never followed by a doubled consonant). Thus *lippes* and *lepes* probably took up roughly equal units of time. Doubled and lengthened consonants have virtually disappeared in Mod.E., except in compounds such as *bell-like, room-mate, un-named* (contrast *unaimed*).
To pronounce a doubled consonant, simply hold the sound longer than usual.

Note: There is some debate about the purpose of doubled consonants in M.E.: what we have said above is simply one school's opinion. Some scholars think the doubling was simply a way of indicating the shortness of the preceding vowel.

12. thritty, bridde, weder
Thritty parfet briddes folwen her fadres thurgh the weder.

Note that many familiar words here metathesized (switched consonant-vowel sequence) since Chaucer's time. Pronounce the sequence as you see it spelled in Chaucer's text.

II. Vowels

General note: The vowels of Chaucer's language are customarily divided into "short" and "long" vowels. The exact quantitative (durational) differences between the two classes are uncertain; we call some vowels long more because they were or have regularly become diphthongs than for any other

sure reason, and other vowels short because they have not diphthongized but
have remained relatively stable over the
centuries. Presumably there must have
been some point of difference among
vowels in M.E. that led to the diph-
thongization of some but not of others.

The so-called short vowels, then, have
changed very little since Chaucer's day.
They were probably a little "tenser"
then than most of them are now: the
i of *this, it,* and *bit* were probably
equally tense in the 14th C. and more
forcefully pronounced (stressed) than
are their modern counterparts; and
the *u* of *up, but,* and *full* would have
been the same—the *u* of *full.* Generally, modern pronunciation is a reliable
guide: vowels not diphthongized in
Mod.E. were generally short in M.E.
Note, however, that a few words having long vowels in M.E., esp. *e* and *o*
(*sleep*-slept) have shortened in Mod.
E.; in M.E. the doubling of a vowel
is a sure sign of a long vowel and, as
in *sleep* (the preterite of *to sleep* in
M.E.), can act as a guide.

Note also that the always unstressed
–*e* found in the decayed inflectional
endings (see above, *Morphology*) had
the sound of *a* in the first syllable of
again, or of *u* in the first syllable of
upon. This so-called "neutral" vowel
sound, however, was in Chaucer's time
given only to the *e* in unaccented final
syllables; it would never have been
pronounced in *again* or *upon* in M.E.,
nor in a host of words whose Mod.E.
versions employ it. The neutral vowel
is generally given the phonetic symbol
(ə).

Because the purpose of this script is to make it easier for you to move from the writing of Chaucer's language to its sounds, we group his vowel sounds in the following pages according to similarities in spelling rather than according to the long-short classification usually employed.

1.a. *a* in that, man, badde, laddre (a)
That man hadde a badde laddre.

In M.E. this *a* probably represents the vowel Americans pronounce in Mod.E. *hot*—but undiphthongized. Generally, sounds having in Mod.E. the *a* of *man, land, cat, hand* had in Middle English the vowel sound of Mod.E. *hot*. In some M.E. words the sound is frequently represented by *o: hond, lond*.

1.b. *a* in name, taken, awaken, caas (a:)
Tak my name in the caas that I awake.

Generally, this M.E. *a* has changed regularly to the diphthong we now pronounce in *name,* etc. (ey). Working backward, we may say that words pronounced with this diphthong in Mod.E. were pronounced with the "simple" long *a* in Chaucer's dialect. The customary M.E. spelling is *a* (without a succeeding doubled consonant, of course; such a doubling would be the sign of a short vowel) or *aa*, as here. In M.E. the sound is exactly the same as short *a* (above) except for duration.

1.c. *au* in cause, laughen, taughten, lawe (au)
How I laughe at the lawes that I cause to ben ytaught.

This diphthong, distinct from that of *thoughte* in M.E., has come to have the same vowel in Mod.E. The distinction made in M.E. is still preserved in the spelling however, and no confusions of the M.E. *au* and *ou* diphthongs are likely. Note that the different diphthongs can occur in two forms of the same word: I *laughe,* but he *lough*.

34

2.a. *i* in this thynne, pynne, inne (ɪ)
      This thynne pynne is inne.

This vowel is virtually the exact equivalent of the stressed *i* in Mod.E. *bit*. In M.E. it is written *i* or *y*. It is the initial *i* of *imitate*—the second *i* of this word has become the neutral vowel (ə) in Mod.E. Be careful not to diphthongize.

2.b. *i* in I, ryden, nye, slye (i:)
      I ryde slye nye.

The long *i* of Chaucer's dialect has changed regularly to the *ai* diphthong we pronounce in Mod.E. *sly, ride*, etc. (ay). Working backward, we may say that Mod.E. words pronounced with the diphthong of *sly* were pronounced with the sound of *seen* (though not diphthongized) in Chaucer's dialect. The usual M.E. spellings, *i, y*, are useful though not infallible guides. Be careful not to diphthongize. Note that in words like *yen* (eyes) and *folye* (folly) *y* and *e* represent *separate syllables.*

3.a. *e* in mette, wedden, gessen, fedden (ɛ)
      They metten, he weddede, I guess he was fedden.

This *e* is almost the exact equivalent of a stressed Mod.E. *e* in *bed* or of the second *e* in *pedestrian* (the first *e* is our neutral vowel again).

3.b. *e* in swete, sleen, fleen, me (e:)
      I se my swete fro me flee.

This sound also has modernized regularly; the words pronounced with the vowel of Mod.E. *see* (unless usually spelled *ea* in Mod.E.; see below) were pronounced in M.E. as here, with an *e* almost like that of Mod.E. *raid*, but without the *i* diphthong. Spelling is *e* or *ee* in M.E. Be careful not to diphthongize.

3.c. *e* in prechen, heeth, heed, deeth (ɛ:)
      Go preche to deeth with youre heed in the heeth.

Another M.E. vowel, though spelled *e, ee*, differed slightly in pronunciation from the *e, ee* of *swete* or *seen*. Words of this other class are regularly spelled with *ea* in Mod.E., as in *heath, breath, preach, meat, break*, etc.; the Mod.E.

35

spelling is a reliable point of difference. *Heath* and *breath* rhyme in Chaucer; their common vowel is lower than the *e* of M.E. *swete*. To make the sound, say M.E. *swete,* as above, but with the jaw held lower, as if you were saying the vowel of Mod.E. *hat.*

3.d. *ey, ai* in daye, saillen, eweye, preyen (εi)

I preye that this daye saille aweye.

This sound has come down to Mod.E. almost but not quite as it was. Though opinion is changeable, the editors of this script agree with the opinion that the M.E. *ai* is *e* as in *bed,* + *i* as in *bit*—as if you were to say *day,* but with the jaw held further open. But the first element of the M.E. sound was almost certainly not as low as the *ai* in Mod.E. *aisle.*

3.e. *ew* in lewed, fewe, shrewen (εu)

I shrewe the lewed fewe.

In a few words whose Mod.E. pronunciation contains the vowel in *lewd,* M.E. employed an *eu* diphthong, as here. In M.E. it is usually spelled *ew.* This diphthong came to be pronounced indistinguishably from those in such words as *knew* and *nature* (see below, 3.f.) around the 15th-16th C. The list of words falling within the class of M.E. *lewed* is short enough to be memorized—and should be, for there is no other easy way to distinguish them from those treated below. They are: *lewed, shewen, fewe, shrewen, hewen* (to hack), *dronklewe, beaute, nevew, leaute.*

3.f. *ew* in knewe, mewe, rewe, newe (iu)

He knewe that he wolde rewe the newe mewe.

This vowel also is spelled *ew* in M.E., and very occasionally *uw,* as in *mewe/muwe.* The presence of the *uw* spelling suggests that this diphthong was still fairly rounded.

4.a. *o* in dogge, hogge, hoppen, hornes (ɔ)

The Mod.E. descendant of this sound varies considerably with dialect. In

The dogge and the hogge hoppen to the hornes.

Eastern New England and standard British the sound is very much the same as the M.E. (ɔ). Elsewhere it may be *a* in some words, ɔ in others, or ɔw in all words. It is probably safest to learn a new vowel. Say the *o* of British *hot* or German *Gott. Do not diphthongize or drawl.*

4.b. *o* in fol, hood, blood (o:)
Whos fols blood is on myn hood?

This sound has a slightly more complex history. Since Chaucer's time, when the vowel was pronounced as in *oh* without diphthong, it has passed through the stages represented in the Mod.E. pronunciation of *food, hood, blood.* What makes working backward difficult is that the change was not a regular one; different words changed at different paces, and frequently older pronunciations lingered on side by side with more modern ones. Thus *blood* may have changed early (15th C. spellings such as *bloud* and *blude* suggest variant pronunciations but also distinct changes from Chaucer's time) but could still be rhymed in the 17th C. with *good* and *mood;* and the whole process of change is still preserved in the three common dialect variants in pronunciation of *roof* (ruwf/ rʊf/ rəf). The characteristic spellings *o* and especially *oo (rofe/roof, rote/ roote/ hod/hood, non/noon)* are especially useful here in isolating the sound. Note also that none of this class of words is still pronounced with the *o* of *holy.*

4.c. *o* in holy, gropen, Pope, rood (ɔ:)
Slowly rood the gropinge pope.

This sound (approximately the vowel of Mod.E. *bawdy*) has changed regularly in most words to the *ou* diphthong we pronounce today in *holy,* etc. (ou). Here too we can argue from our present sound to the most probable M.E. sound. The sound is written *o* + consonant + vowel, as in *holy;* or *oo,* as in *rood.* But remember that other M.E. sounds also can be represented by *o* or *oo:* the surest guide to this class is the Mod.E. pronunciation—if the word now has the vowel of Mod.E. *holy,* it had in Chaucer's time approximately the vowel of *bawdy.*

4.d. *ow* in knowen, growen, lowe (ou)

He that knoweth groweth lowe.

The written diphthong *ow* frequently appears to be an effort to indicate a M.E. diphthong substantially the same as the one we pronounce in such words as *low.* This sound has changed little. Note, however, that another M.E. sound, also indicated by *ou* or *ow,* has become our Mod.E. *fowls.* (See 5.b. below.) If you keep in mind the Mod.E. pronunciation, you cannot confuse the two.

4.e. *ou* in foughten, thoughten, boughten (ɔu)

They foughte, he thoughte, I boughte hit.

This diphthong, once distinct from that of *cause,* has come to the same thing in Mod.E. In Chaucer's language, the two are still distinct. The presence of *gh* or of its variant spelling *h* (ç) after the diphthong marks it off absolutely from the diphthong of Mod.E. *loud.*

5.a. *u* in yong, love, lusten, sonne (ʊ)

The yonge love lusteth after sonne.

This *u* (now generally given the vowel of Mod.E. *hut*) had the vowel sound of Mod.E. *full* in Chaucer's time. Note the spelling: in M.E. short *u* is frequently spelled *o,* as here in *yong,* etc., but is *never* spelled *oo* or *ou.* The general rule is that a word whose Mod.E. pronunciation yields the neutral vowel (the *u* of *hut, cut, but,* etc.) had in Chaucer's time the *u* of *full,* with the lips perhaps a little more rounded and the stress stronger.

5.b. *u* in loud, thow, sounen, foweles (u:)

Thow sounest loudere than oure foweles doon.

This vowel has changed regularly in Mod.E. to the diphthong of *round*. Backward logic will help us. So will the characteristic spellings, *ou* and *ow*. Note, however, that these spellings are not definitive evidence by themselves, *ou* and *ow* being also used to represent other M.E. sounds.

5.c. *u* in suster, justise, murye (y)

The justise of my suster is murye.

South and west of London many words of French origin and also a special class of O.E. words evidently were pronounced with a short *u* much like that of Mod. French *humble*. This sound has completely vanished from Mod.E. To make the sound: say *ee!* with the tongue and *oo!* with the lips. The history of this sound in Chaucer's dialect can afford a good illustration of the kind of reconstruction of his phonological system that has been more easily, less hazardously carried through for other sounds. Although Chaucer usually employs the standard East Midland form, in which the rounded *u* of O.E. and of O.F. (the sounds doubtless were slightly different, originally, but here may be treated as one) had changed to *i,* Chaucer also occasionally uses a spelling indicating either that in some words his dialect regularly preserved the rounded *u* vowel derived from O.E. or from O.F., or that he deliberately chose a variant dialect pronunciation readily available to him. In fact, Chaucer fairly frequently uses dialect forms uncommon in the East Midlands, probably because such forms circulated commonly in London, which was very near the Southern and West Midland dialect areas. Thus in the Gen. Prol. Chaucer uses *mury,*

5.d. *u* in aventures, creature, nature,
pure (y:) (iu)

The aventures of swych creatures
in nature ben pure.

mery, and *myrie* within the same 100 lines. This word, therefore, was probably somewhat rounded. Mod.E. *sin,* however, regularly *synne* or *sunne* in Southern dialect, is rhymed by Chaucer with *inne* and spelled only *synne* or *sinne*—never *sunne.* Doubtless it, therefore, had unrounded in London dialect in Chaucer's time. Generally words pronounced or spelled with *i* in Mod.E. but spelled in Chaucer with *u* (*suster*) probably were pronounced with a slightly rounded *u.* It is also probable that in recently borrowed French words such as *humble, justise,* the vowel was still rounded and tense. But both the long and the short *u* of this type were certainly lost in London speech during this period, if not before. In another small class of words borrowed largely from French, M.E. preserved a long tense *u,* like the *u* of Mod. French *pur* (oo! with the lips, ee! with the tongue), which later changed in the North and East Midlands to an *iu* diphthong like the one we pronounce in Mod.E. *pure.* There is debate about whether Chaucer employed the French *u* or the *iu* diphthong. Fr. *u* had certainly changed to *iu* in London by the end of the 15th C. and probably was changed to *iu* during Chaucer's lifetime, if not before. But Chaucer appears to have preserved some "older" features of his dialect for poetic purposes, and may have done so here; further, he was a court poet and French was a second language at court. He rhymes these words only with words of the same provenance and type: *creature, ordure, assure, stature, noriture, sepulture,* etc.

1.　　Me thoghte thus: that hyt was May,

　　And in the dawenynge I lay
　　(Me mette thus) in my bed al naked,

　　And loked forth, for I was waked
　　With smale foules a gret hep

　　That had affrayed me out of my slep,
　　Thorgh noyse and swetnesse of her song.

　　And, as me mette, they sate among
　　Upon my chambre roof wythoute,
　　Upon the tyles, overal aboute,

　　And songen, everych in hys wyse,
　　The moste solempne servise
　　By noote, that ever man, y trowe,
　　Had herd; for som of hem song lowe,
　　Som high, and al of oon acord.

　　To telle shortly, att oo word,
　　Was never herd so swete a steven,—
　　But hyt had be a thyng of heven,—

2.　　With that me thoghte that this kyng
　　Gan homwardes for to ryde
　　Unto a place, was there besyde,
　　Which was from us but a lyte.

　　A long castel with walles white,
　　Be seynt Johan! on a ryche hil
　　As me mette; but thus hyt fil.

　　Ryght thus me mette, as I yow telle,
　　That in the castell ther was a belle,
　　As hyt hadde smyten houres twelve.—

　　Therwyth I awook myselve
　　And fond me lyinge in my bed;

41

And the book that I hadde red,
Of Alcione and Seys the kyng,
And of the goddes of slepyng,
I fond hyt in myn hond ful even.

3. The day gan faylen, and the derke nyght,
That reveth bestes from here besynesse,
Berafte me my bok for lak of lyght,

And to my bed I gan me for to dresse,
Fulfyld of thought and busy hevynesse;

For bothe I hadde thyng which that I nolde,
And ek I nadde that thyng that I wolde.

* * *

The wery huntere, slepynge in his bed,
To wode ayeyn his mynde goth anon;

The juge dremeth how his plees been sped;
The cartere dremeth how his cartes gon;
The riche, of gold; the knyght fyght with his fon;

The syke met he drynketh of the tonne;
The lover met he hath his lady wonne.

4. And for these water-foules tho began
The goos to speke, and in hire kakelynge
She seyde, "Pes! now tak kep every man,

And herkeneth which a resoun I shal forth brynge!
My wit is sharp, I love no taryinge;

I seye I rede hym, though he were my brother,
But she wol love hym, lat hym love another!"

"Lo, here a parfit resoun of a goos!"
Quod the sperhauk; "Nevere mot she thee!

Lo, swich it is to have a tonge loos!
Now, parde! fol, yit were it bed for the
Han holde thy pes than shewed thy nycete.

It lyth nat in his wit, ne in his wille,
But soth is seyd, 'a fol can not be stille!'"

5. "Now welcome, somer, with thy sonne softe,
   That hast this wintres wedres overshake,
   And driven away the longe nyghtes blake!

   "Saynt Valentyn, that art ful hy on-lofte,
   Thus syngen smale foules for thy sake:
   Now welcome, somer, with thy sonne softe,
   That hast this wintres wedres overshake.

   "Wel han they cause for to gladen ofte,
   Sith ech of hem recovered hath hys make,
   Ful blissful mowe they synge when they wake

   Now welcome, somer, with thy sonne softe,
   That hast this wintres wedres overshake,
   And driven away the longe nyghtes blake!"

SELECTIONS FROM *Troilus and Criseyde*

1.   The double sorwe of Troilus to tellen,
      That was the kyng Priamus sone of Troye,

      In lovynge, how his aventures fellen
      Fro wo to wele, and after out of joie,
      My purpos is, er that I parte fro ye.

      Thesiphone, thow help me for t'endite
      Thise woful vers, that wepen as I write.

      To the clepe I, thow goddesse of torment,
      Thow cruwel Furie, sorwynge evere yn peyne,

      Help me, that am the sorwful instrument,
      That helpeth loveres, as I kan, to pleyne.

      For wel sit it, the sothe for to seyne,
      A woful wight to han a drery feere,
      And to a sorwful tale, a sory chere.

      For I, that God of Loves servantz serve,
      Ne dar to Love, for myn unliklynesse,
      Preyen for speed, al sholde I therfore sterve,
      So fer am I from his help in derknesse.

43

But natheles, if this may don gladnesse.
To any lovere, and his cause availle,
Have he my thonk, and myn be this travaille!

2. Lay al this mene while Troilus,
Recordyng his lesson in this manere:

"Mafay," thoughte he, "thus wol I say, and thus;
Thus wol I pleyne unto my lady dere;
That word is good, and this shal be my cheere;

This nyl I nought foryeten in no wise."
God leve hym werken as he kan devyse!

And lord, so that his herte gan to quappe,
Heryng hire come, and shorte for to sike!

And Pandarus, that ledde hire by the lappe,
Com ner, and gan in at the curtyn pike,
And seyde, "God do boot on alle syke!

Se who is here yow comen to visite;
Lo, here is she that is youre deth to wite."

Therwith it semed as he wepte almost.

"Ha, a," quod Troilus so reufully,
"Wher me be wo, O myghty God, thow woost!
Who is al ther? I se nought trewely,"

"Sire," quod Criseyde, "it is Pandare and I."
"Ye, swete herte? allas, I may nought rise,
To knele and do yow honour in som wyse."

And dressed hym upward, and she right tho
Gan bothe hire hondes softe upon hym leye.

"O, for the love of God, do ye nought so
To me," quod she, "I! what is this to seye?

Sire, comen am I to yow for causes tweye:
First, yow to thonke, and of youre lordship eke
Continuance I wolde yow biseke."

44

This Troilus, that herde his lady preye
Of lordshipe hym, wax neither quyk ne ded,
Ne myghte o word for shame to it seye,
Although men sholde smyten of his hed.

But, Lord, so he wex sodeynliche red,
And sire, his lessoun, that he wende konne
To preyen hire, is thorugh his wit ironne.

3. "Myn alderlevest Lord, and brother deere,

God woot, and thow, that it sat me so soore,
When I the saugh so langwisshyng to-yere
For love, of which thi wo wax alwey moore,

That I, with al my myght and al my loore,
Have evere sithen don my bisynesse
To brynge the to joye out of distresse,

"And have it brought to swich plit as thow woost,
So that thorugh me thow stondest now in weye to faren wel:

I sey it for no bost,
And wostow whi? for shame it is to seye:

For the have I bigonne a gamen pleye,
Which that I nevere do shal eft for other,
Although he were a thousand fold my brother.

"That is to seye, for the am I bicomen,
Bitwixen game and ernest, swich a meene
As maken wommen unto men to comen;

Al sey I nought, thow wost wel what I meene.

For the have I my nece, of vices cleene,
So fully maad thi gentilesse triste,
That al shal ben right as thiselven liste.

4. Swich fyn hath, lo, this Troilus for love!
Swich fyn hath al his grete worthynesse!

Swich fyn hath his estat real above,
Swich fyn his lust, swich fyn hath his noblesse!
Swich fyn hath false worldes brotelnesse!

45

And thus began his lovyng of Criseyde
As I have told, and in this wise he deyde.

O yonge, fresshe folkes, he or she,
In which that love up groweth with youre age,
Repeyreth hom fro worldly vanyte,

And of youre herte up casteth the visage
To thilke God that after his ymage
Yow made, and thynketh al nys but a faire
This world, that passeth soone as floures faire.

And loveth hym, the which that right for love
Upon a crois, oure soules for to beye,
First starf, and roos, and sit in hevene above;

For he nyl falsen no wight, dar I seye,
That wol his herte al holly on hym leye.

And syn he best to love is, and most meke,
What nedeth feynede loves for to seke?

Lo here, of payens corsed olde rites,
Lo here, what alle hire goddes may availle;
Lo here, thise wrecched worldes appetites;

Lo here, the fyn and guerdoun for travaille
Of Jove, Appollo, of Mars, of swich rascaille!

Lo here, the forme of olde clerkis speche
In poetrie, if ye hire bokes seche.

SELECTIONS FROM THE *Canterbury Tales,* Series I

1.   Whan that Aprill with his shoures soote
The droghte of March hath perced to the roote,

And bathed every veyne in swich licour
Of which vertu engendred is the flour;

Whan Zephirus eek with his sweete breeth
Inspired hath in every holt and heeth
The tendre croppes,

                    and the yonge sonne
hath in the Ram his halve cours yronne,

And smale foweles maken melodye,
That slepen al the nyght with open ye
(So priketh hem nature in hir corages);

Thanne longen folk to goon on pilgrimages,
And palmeres for to seken straunge strondes,
To ferne halwes, kowthe in sondry londes;

And specially from every shires ende
Of Engelond to Caunterbury they wende,
The hooly blisful martir for to seke,
That hem hath holpen whan that they were seeke.
                    (From the "General Prologue")

2.   Ther saugh I first the derke ymaginyng
       Of Felonye, and al the compassying;

The crueel Ire, reed as any gleede;
The pykepurs, and eek the pale Drede;

The smylere with the knyf under the cloke;
The shepne brennynge with the blake smoke;

The tresoun of the mordrynge in the bedde;
The open werre, with woundes al bibledde;

Contek, with blody knyf and sharp manace.
Al ful of chirkyng was that sory place.

The sleere of hymself yet saugh I ther—
His herte-blood hath bathed al his heer;

The nayl ydryven in the shode a-nyght;
The colde deeth, with mouth gapyng upright.

Amyddes of the temple sat Meschaunce,
With disconfort and sory contenaunce.

Yet saugh I Woodnesse, laughynge in his rage,
Armed Compleint, Outhees, and fiers Outrage;

The careyne in the busk, with throte ycorve;
A thousand slayn, and nat of qualm ystorve;

The tiraunt, with the pray by force yraft;
The toun destroyed, ther was no thyng laft.

Yet saugh I brent the shippes hoppesteres;
The hunte strangled with the wilde beres;

The sowe freten the child right in the cradel;
The cook yscalded, for al his longe ladel.

Noght was foryeten by the infortune of Marte
The cartere overryden with his carte;
Under the wheel ful lowe he lay adoun.
                    (From "The Knight's Tale")

3. Thanne seyde he thus as ye shal after heere:
   "Naught may the woful spirit in myn herte
   Declare o point of alle my sorwes smerte
   To yow, my lady, that I love moost;

   But I biquethe the servyce of my goost
   To you aboven every creature,
   Syn that my lyf may no lenger dure.

   Allas, the wo! allas, the peynes stronge,
   That I for yow have suffred, and so longe!

   Allas, the deeth! allas, myn Emelye!
   Allas, departynge of oure compaignye!

   Allas myn hertes queene! allas, my wyf!
   Myn hertes lady, endere of my lyf!

   What is this world? what asketh men to have
   Now with his love, now in his colde grave
   Allone, withouten any compaignye.
                    (From "The Knight's Tale")

4. "What do ye, hony-comb, sweete Alisoun,
   My faire bryd, my sweete cynamome?
   Awaketh, lemman myn, and speketh to me!

Wel litel thynken ye upon my wo,
That for youre love I swete there I go.

No wonder is thogh that I swelte and swete;
I moorne as dooth a lamb after the tete.

Ywis, lemman, I have swich love-longynge,
That lik a turtel trewe is my moornynge.
I may nat ete na moore than a mayde."

   "Go fro the wyndow, Jakke fool," she sayde;
"As help me God, it wol nat be 'com pa me!
I love another—and elles I were to blame—
Wel bet than thee, by Jhesu, Absolon.

Go forth thy wey, or I wol caste a ston,
And lat me slepe, a twenty devel wey!"

   "Allas," quod Absolon, "and weylawey,
That trewe love was evere so yvel biset!

Thanne kysse me, syn it may be no bet,
For Jhesus love, and for the love of me."

   "Wiltow thanne go thy wey therwith?" quod she.
"Ye, certes, lemman," quod this Absolon.
"Thanne make thee redy," quod she, "I come anon."
                    (From "The Reeve's Tale")

5.   "It shal be doon" quod Symkyn, "by my fay!
What wol ye doon whil that it is in hande?"

   "By God, right by the hopur wil I stande,"
Quod John, "and se howgates the corn gas in.

Yet saugh I nevere, by my fader kyn,
How that the hopur wagges til and fra."

   Aleyn answerde, "John, and wiltow swa?

Thanne wil I be bynethe, by my croun,
And se how that the mele falles doun
Into the trough; that sal be my disport.

49

For John, y-faith, I may been of youre sort;
I is as ille a millere as ar ye."
(From "The Reeve's Tale")

SELECTIONS FROM THE *Canterbury Tales,* Series II

1.   In th' olde dayes of the Kyng Arthour,
Of which that Britons speken greet honour,
Al was this land fulfild of fayerye.

The elf-queene, with hir joly compaignye,
Daunced ful ofte in many a grene mede.

This was the olde opinion, as I rede;
I speke of manye hundred yeres ago.

But now kan no man se none elves mo,
For now the grete charitee and prayeres
Of lymytours and othere hooly freres,

That serchen every lond and every streem,
As thikke as motes in the sonne-beem,

Blessynge halles, chambres, kichenes, boures,
Citees, burghes, castels, hye toures,
Thropes, bernes, shipnes, dayeryes—
This maketh that ther ben no fayeryes.

For ther as wont to walken was an elf,
Ther walketh now the lymytour hymself
In undermeles and in morwenynges,

And seyth his matyns and his hooly thynges
As he gooth in his lymytacioun.

Wommen may go now saufly up and doun.
In every bussh or under every tree
Ther is noon oother incubus but he,
And he ne wol doon hem but dishonour.
(From "The Wife of Bath's Tale")

2.   Whan they han goon nat fully half a mile,
Right as they wolde han troden over a stile,
An oold man and a povre with hem mette.

This olde man ful mekely hem grette,
And seyde thus, "Now, lordes, God you see!"

The proudeste of thise riotoures three
Answerde agayn, "What, carl, with sory grace!
Why artow al forwrapped save thy face?
Why lyvestow so longe in so greet age?"

This olde man gan looke in his visage,
And seyde thus: "For I ne kan nat fynde
A man, though that I walked into Ynde,
Neither in citee ne in no village,
That wolde change his youthe for myn age;

"And therfore moot I han myn age stille,
As longe tyme as it is Goddes wille.

"Ne Deeth, allas! ne wol nat han my lyf
Thus walke I, lyk a resteless kaityf,
And on the ground, which is my moodres gate,
I knokke with my staf, bothe erly and late,
And seye 'Leeve mooder, leet me in!
Lo how I vanysshe, flessh, and blood, and skyn!
Allas! whan shul my bones been at reste?' "

(From "The Pardoner's Tale")

3.   This sely wydwe and eek hir doghtres two
Herden thise hennes crie and maken wo,

And out at dores stirten they anon,
And syen the fox toward the grove gon,
And bar upon his bak the cok away,

And cryden, "Out! harrow! and weylaway!
Ha! Ha! the fox!" and after hym they ran,
And eek with staves many another man.

Ran Colle oure dogge, and Talbot and Gerland,
And Malkyn, with a dystaf in hir hand;

Ran cow and calf, and eek the verray hogges,
So fered for the berkyng of the dogges
And shoutyng of the men and wommen eeke,
They ronne so hem thoughte hir herte breeke.

They yolleden as feendes doon in helle;
The dokes cryden as men wolde hem quelle;

The gees for feere flowen over the trees;
Out of the hyve cam the swarm of bees.
So hydous was the noyse, a, benedicitee!

Certes, he Jakke Straw and his meynee
Ne made nevere shoutes half so shrille
Whan that they wolden any Flemyng kille,
As thilke day was maad upon the fox.

(From "The Nun's Priest's Tale")

4.   Now preye I to hem alle that herkne this litel tretys or rede, that if ther be any thyng in it that liketh hem, that therof they thanken oure Lord Jhesu Christ, of whom procedeth al wit and al goodnesse.

And if ther be any thyng that displese hem, I preye hem also that they arrette it to the defaute of myn unkonnynge, and nat to my wyl, that wolde ful fayn have seyd bettre if I hadde had konnynge.

For oure book seith, "Al that is writen is writen for oure doctrine," and that is myn entente.

Wherfore I biseke yow mekely, for the mercy of God, that ye preye for me that Crist have mercy on me and foryeve me my giltes;

and namely of my translacions and enditynges of worldly vanitees, the whiche I revoke in my retracciouns:

as is the book of Troilus; the book also of Fame; the book of the xxv. Ladies; the book of the Duchesse; the book of Seint Valentynes day of the Parlement of Briddes; the tales of Caunterbury, thilke that sownen into synne;

the book of the Leoun; and many another book, if they were in my remembrance, and many a song and many a leccherous lay;

(From the Conclusion of the "Canterbury Tales")